Where Are The Fishers of Men? The Great Commission:

Lost in the Crowd!

Self-Published by
Alisa L. Grace
Sanford, FL 32771

ISBN: 978-1-966129-52-3

First Edition

Printed in the United States of America

Library of Congress Cataloging-in-Publication Data

Grace, Alisa L.

Title of the Book: Where Are the Fishers of Men? The Great Commission: Lost in the Crowd!

Library of Congress Control Number: 2024925235

Disclaimer: The views expressed in this book are those of the author and do not necessarily reflect any organizations or individuals mentioned.

Acknowledgments: The author wishes to thank God, Her Husband (Linion), Victory Temple of God, Florida SPECS, Unity Youth Association, All About Serving You, Angels-ANJ Events, NordeVest, and Love & Create Life for their support and contributions.x

Dedication:

This book is dedicated to all the faithful disciples of Christ who have answered His call to "go and make disciples." May you continue to be fishers of men, spreading His love and truth to a world in need. This is also dedicated to the pastors, leaders, and church members who long to see revival and renewal within the body of Christ. Your faithfulness to the Great Commission is a beacon of hope and transformation.

Why Read This Book?

Are you longing for something more in your Christian walk? Do you sense a disconnect between your church's bustling activity and the heart of Christ's commission? Do you yearn for a deeper, more authentic faith that transforms lives and impacts the world?

If so, then this book is for you.

"Where Are The Fishers of Men? The Great Commission: Lost in the Crowd!" is a compelling and heartfelt call to rediscover the true essence of discipleship and reclaim the church's mission to make disciples of all nations.

Here's why you should read this book:

To Rekindle Your Passion for Christ: This book will re-ignite your love for Jesus and inspire you to pursue a deeper relationship with Him.

To Understand True Discipleship: You'll clearly understand what it means to be a disciple, not just a church member.

To Challenge the Status Quo: This book dares to question the comfortable Christianity that often permeates our churches.

To Discover Your Role in God's Kingdom: You'll be empowered to embrace your unique calling and actively participate in God's redemptive plan.

To Be Equipped for Ministry: You'll learn to effectively share your faith, disciple others, and serve those in need.

To Find Hope and Inspiration: This book offers a refreshing perspective on the church and its potential to impact the world.

This book is for you if:

- ☐ You are a pastor seeking to lead your congregation toward authentic discipleship.

- ☐ You are a church member longing for a deeper connection with Christ and a more meaningful church experience.

- ☐ You are concerned about the direction of the church and its effectiveness in fulfilling the Great Commission.

- ☐ You seek to grow in your faith and make a real difference.

"Where Are the Fishers of Men?" is not just another book about church growth or Christian living. It is a prophetic call to return to the heart of the Gospel and reclaim the church's mission to make disciples. It will challenge, inspire, and equip you to be a fisher of men in a world desperately in need of Christ's love.

How to Use This Book

Dear reader,

This book invites you on a personal journey of rediscovery, guiding you back to the heart of Christ's commission for His Church. It's a call for you to examine your heart, reevaluate your priorities, and realign yourself with the biblical discipleship model.

To truly engage with the transformative message of this book, you should approach it with an open mind and a receptive heart. Here are some suggestions to enhance your reading experience:

Pray: Before you dive into each chapter, take a moment to invite the Holy Spirit to guide your understanding and illuminate the truths in these pages. Open your heart to what He might reveal to you.

Reflect: After each section, pause to consider the concepts presented. Think about how they apply to your life, church, and relationship with Christ. What resonates with you?

Discuss: Share your insights with others. Talk about what you've learned with fellow believers, your pastor, or in a small group. Engaging in conversation can deepen your understanding and inspire you to take action.

Journal: Keep a notebook handy to jot down your thoughts, questions, and personal revelations. The companion journal, "The Great Commission Challenge: 30 Days to Transformation," offers a structured way to process and apply the book's message to your daily life.

Act: Remember, this isn't just a book to read; it's an opportunity for action. Look for ways to share your faith, disciple others, and serve those in need. Let this journey inspire you to make a meaningful difference in your life and the lives of others.

Structure of the Book

This book is divided into five parts, each designed to guide you through a critical aspect of the Great Commission and its implications for your journey in the modern church.

Part 1: Disciples vs. Members

In this section, you'll explore what it truly means to be a disciple. You'll find a stark contrast between a living, vibrant discipleship and the passive membership mentality that often permeates our churches today. As you reflect on the characteristics of a genuine disciple, you will be challenged to commit fully to your relationship with Christ.

Part 2: Fishers of Men vs. Hirelings

Here, you'll dive into the biblical vision of what it means to be a pastor as a shepherd and recognize the potential pitfalls of self-serving leaders. You'll learn to identify true shepherds and appreciate the significance of nurturing a healthy relationship between you and your spiritual leaders.

Part 3: Sheep vs. Consumers

This part encourages you to embrace your role as an active participant in the body of Christ rather than adopting a consumer mindset that often creeps into church life. You will be invited to reflect on your responsibilities and how you can actively contribute to the community around you.

Part 4: Christ, the Head of the Church

This section reminds you that Christ is supreme as the Head of the Church, not any pastor or denomination. You'll be challenged to place Jesus' teachings at the forefront of your life and to seek the guidance of the Holy Spirit in all your decisions.

Part 5: The Church's Mission: Making Disciples

Finally, this part calls you—and the church—back to its primary mission: making disciples. You'll be encouraged to engage in evangelism, discipleship, and active service to others, embracing your unique role in fulfilling the Great Commission.

As you journey through each part, you are not just reading; you're being invited to grow, challenge yourself, and actively live out your faith in a way that impacts those around you.

Chapter Format

Each chapter will begin with an explanation of its focus and end with:

> **Transformative Questions:** Three thought-provoking questions to help you apply the chapter's message to your life.

> **Prayer Prompt:** A suggestion for a specific prayer related to the chapter's theme.

Companion Journal

At the end of the book, you will find an introduction to the companion journal, "The Great Commission Challenge: 30 Days to Transformation." This journal provides a 30-day challenge designed to help you deepen your understanding of the book's message and integrate it into your daily life.

Let us begin this journey together, seeking the truth in love and allowing the Holy Spirit to guide us to the heart of Christ's commission.

Contents

Introduction

Beloved brothers and sisters, a question burns in our hearts that echoes through the ages and whispers on the winds of the Spirit: **Where are the fishers of men?** Where are those who, like the old disciples, will leave everything to follow Jesus, embrace His teachings, and cast their nets wide into the sea of humanity, drawing souls to His loving embrace?

The air we breathe seems to vibrate with a holy discontent, a yearning for something more than the status quo. We see bustling churches, packed pews, and impressive programs, yet a nagging question lingers: Are we genuinely fulfilling the Great Commission? Are we making disciples who passionately pursue Christ or simply gathering members to fill our buildings?

The scriptures vividly depict what it means to be a fisher of men. In Matthew 4:19, Jesus calls Simon and Andrew, "Follow me, and **I will make you fishers of men**." Mark 1:17 echoes this call, with Jesus proclaiming, "Come, follow me, and **I will send you out to fish for people**." Luke 5:10-11 shows us the disciples leaving everything—their boats, nets, livelihoods—to follow Jesus. In Matthew 8:22, Jesus challenges a would-be follower to prioritize the Kingdom of God above all else. And in John 21:19, Jesus lovingly instructs Peter, **"Feed my sheep,"** emphasizing the shepherd's heart for his flock.

These passages reveal a profound truth: following Jesus demands total commitment. It requires a willingness to leave behind the familiar and embrace a life of radical obedience, selfless service, and passionate devotion to His mission. It's a call to be more than just a church member; it's a call to be a disciple, a fisher of men, a vessel through which God's love and power can flow to a lost and hurting world.

This book, dear friends, is not a condemnation of the church. It is a love letter penned with a heart overflowing with concern and hope. It is a gentle invitation to reexamine our ways, rediscover the Gospel's heart, and realign ourselves with Christ's original commission. It is a call to invite the Holy Spirit back into our midst, to allow Him to move freely and powerfully, transforming lives and restoring the church to its rightful place as a beacon of hope and healing in a broken world.

Our heavenly Father longs to work through us, not as a genie granting wishes, but as willing partners in His redemptive plan. He desires to see His church ablaze with His glory, a place where the sick are healed, the lost are found, the brokenhearted are comforted, and the hungry are fed. He yearns to see His children living as faithful disciples, reflecting His love and compassion to a world desperately in need.

This is not a pipe dream, beloved. It is the very heart of the Gospel. It is why Jesus came, lived, died, and rose again. It is the mission He entrusted to His followers, which continues today.

Let us, together, embark on this journey of rediscovery. Let us delve into the scriptures, examine our hearts, and allow the Holy Spirit to guide us back to the true essence of discipleship. Let us reclaim the Great Commission, not as a burden but as a joyous privilege, a sacred responsibility, and an extraordinary adventure.

Let us become fishers of men, casting our nets wide and drawing souls into the loving embrace of our Savior. Let us be Jesus' hands and feet, extending His grace and mercy to a world yearning for hope. Let us be the church He intended us to be, a radiant light shining brightly in the darkness, a beacon of love and truth that draws all people to Him.

Come, let us begin.

Part 1:
Disciples vs. Members

In this section, we will embark on a journey to rediscover the true meaning of discipleship. We will delve into the Scriptures to understand what it truly means to follow Jesus and how this differs from simply being a church member. Prepare to be challenged and inspired as we explore the transformative power of authentic discipleship.

Chapter 1:
Defining Discipleship

What does it mean to be a disciple of Jesus Christ? Is it merely attending church services, participating in activities, and identifying with a particular denomination? Or is there something more, something deeper, something that calls for a radical transformation of our hearts and lives?

The Scriptures paint a vivid picture of discipleship. It is a learning journey to grow and become more like Christ. It is a lifelong commitment to follow Jesus, embrace His teachings, and live a life that reflects His love and compassion.

In Luke 14:26-27, Jesus Himself sets the standard for discipleship: "If anyone comes to me and does not hate father and mother, wife and children, brothers and sisters—yes, even their own life—such a person cannot be my disciple. And whoever does not carry their cross and follow me cannot be my disciple." These words may seem harsh at first glance, but they reveal the depth of commitment required to follow Jesus.

True discipleship demands a willingness to surrender our desires, ambitions, and even our closest relationships to prioritize our relationship with Christ. It calls for a life of self-denial, taking up our cross daily and following Jesus, no matter the cost.

Discipleship is not a passive endeavor. It is an active pursuit of Christ, a constant striving to grow in our knowledge of Him and to conform our lives to His image. It is a transformative journey that leads to a deeper relationship with God, a greater understanding of His Word, and a more passionate commitment to His mission.

Transformative Questions:

1. What does Jesus' call to discipleship in Luke 14:26-27 reveal about the commitment required to follow Him?

_____

_____

_____

2. In what ways have you prioritized your relationship with Christ above other relationships and pursuits in your life?

_____

_____

_____

3. How can you actively pursue a deeper relationship with Jesus and grow your understanding of His teachings?

_____

_____

_____

Prayer Prompt:

Pray that God would give you a deeper understanding of what it means to be a disciple of Jesus Christ. Ask Him to help you prioritize your relationship with Him above all else and to live a life that reflects His love and compassion.

Chapter 2:
The Marks of a Disciple

How can we recognize a true disciple of Jesus Christ? What distinguishes them from the crowd? The Scriptures provide several vital indicators of authentic discipleship.

Obedience to Christ's Commands: Jesus Himself said, "If you love me, keep my commands" (John 14:15). True disciples demonstrate their love for Jesus by obeying His teachings and living according to His Word.

Bearing Fruit: In John 15:8, Jesus declares, "This is to my Father's glory, that you bear much fruit, showing yourselves to be my disciples." True disciples bear fruit in their lives, exhibiting the qualities of the Spirit: love, joy, peace, patience, kindness, goodness, faithfulness, gentleness, and self-control (Galatians 5:22-23).

Love for One Another: Jesus said, "A new command I give you: Love one another. As I have loved you, so you must love one another. By this, everyone will know that you are my disciples if you love one another" (John 13:34-35). True disciples demonstrate genuine love and compassion for their fellow believers, extending grace, forgiveness, and support.

Evangelism: In Matthew 28:19-20, Jesus commissions His disciples to "go and make disciples of all nations." True disciples actively share the Gospel and make disciples, fulfilling the Great Commission.

These are just a few marks that distinguish true disciples of Jesus Christ. They are not perfect but strive to live lives that honor and glorify God. They are committed to growing in their faith, serving others, and sharing the good news of salvation with the world.

Transformative Questions:

1. In what ways are you actively obeying Christ's commands and living according to His Word?

   _____

   _____

   _____

2. What kind of fruit is evident in your life due to your relationship with Jesus?

   _____

   _____

   _____

3. How are you demonstrating love for your fellow believers and sharing the Gospel with those who do not yet know Christ?

   _____

   _____

   _____

Prayer Prompt:

Pray that God will help you cultivate the marks of a true disciple in your life. Ask Him to fill you with His Spirit and empower you to live a life that honors Him and draws others to Him.

Appendix: Tools for Transformation

This appendix provides practical resources to help individuals and churches realign with the Great Commission. Whether you seek personal spiritual growth, leading a church, or fostering unity among believers, these tools encourage and equip you to make disciples.

Chapter 3:
The Membership Mentality

In today's church culture, there is a subtle but dangerous trend toward prioritizing church attendance and membership over genuine discipleship. This "membership mentality" can lead to a passive, consumeristic approach to faith, hindering spiritual growth and the fulfillment of the Great Commission.

The danger of the membership mentality lies in its focus on outward appearances rather than inward transformation. It can create a false sense of security, leading people to believe that simply being a church member is enough to guarantee their salvation. However, Jesus Himself warned against this mindset in Matthew 7:21-23, saying, "Not everyone who says to me, 'Lord, Lord,' will enter the kingdom of heaven, but only the one who does the will of my Father who is in heaven."

The membership mentality can also hinder the fulfillment of the Great Commission. The church can become inward-focused and complacent when attracting and retaining members rather than making disciples. This can lead to a lack of passion for evangelism and a reluctance to step outside our comfort zones to share the Gospel with others.

Furthermore, the consumeristic mindset prevalent in some churches can further exacerbate the problem. When people view the church as a service provider rather than a community of believers, they may become more concerned with their needs and preferences than serving others and advancing God's kingdom.

We must recognize the dangers of the membership mentality and actively resist its influence. We must shift our focus from being church members to becoming true disciples of Jesus Christ. This requires a commitment to actively pursuing a deeper relationship with God, growing in our knowledge of His Word, and living lives that reflect His love and compassion.

Transformative Questions:

1. In what ways have you observed the "membership mentality" in your own life or your church?

   _____

   _____

   _____

2. How can you resist the consumeristic mindset and prioritize serving others and advancing God's kingdom?

   _____

   _____

   _____

3. What steps can you take to cultivate a deeper relationship with God and grow your understanding of His Word?

   _____

   _____

   _____

Prayer Prompt:

Pray that God will help you avoid the trap of the membership mentality and embrace the transformative power of true discipleship. Ask Him to give you a passion for His Word, a heart for service, and a boldness to share the Gospel with others.

Part 2:
Fishers of Men vs. Hirelings

---

*In this section, we will explore the crucial distinction
between true shepherds, who embody the heart of Christ, and
hirelings, who may prioritize their interests above the flock's
needs. We will examine the biblical role of a pastor and
learn how to discern those who genuinely lead with love and
sacrifice.*

Chapter 4:
The Shepherd's Heart

Jesus, our Good Shepherd, exemplified the true essence of pastoral leadership. He laid down His life for His sheep, demonstrating the ultimate act of love and sacrifice. In John 10:11, He declares, "I am the good shepherd. The good shepherd lays down his life for the sheep." This selfless devotion forms the foundation of a shepherd's heart.

Following in Jesus's footsteps, a faithful shepherd prioritizes the flock's well-being above personal gain or ambition. Their heart beats in rhythm with the heart of the Father, seeking to nourish, guide, and protect those entrusted to their care.

> **Feeding the Sheep:** Just as a shepherd nourishes their sheep, a pastor feeds the flock with the Word of God. This involves diligently studying and accurately teaching the Scriptures, equipping the saints for ministry work, and nurturing their spiritual growth. As Peter instructs in 1 Peter 5:2, "Be shepherds of God's flock that is under your care, watching over them—not because you must, but because you are willing, as God wants you to be; not pursuing dishonest gain, but eager to serve."

Guiding the Sheep: A shepherd guides their sheep to green pastures and still waters. Similarly, a pastor provides spiritual direction, offering wise counsel and leading the flock toward a deeper relationship with Christ. Proverbs 27:23 reminds us, "Be sure you know the condition of your flocks; give careful attention to your herds."

> **Protecting the Sheep:** A shepherd protects their sheep from predators and dangers. Likewise, a pastor safeguards the flock from false teachings, harmful influences, and spiritual attacks. Ezekiel 34:2-4 speaks to the shepherds who neglect this duty: "Woe to you shepherds of Israel who only take care of yourselves! Should not shepherds take care of the flock? You eat the curds, clothe yourselves with the wool, and slaughter the choice animals, but you do not take care of the flock. You have not strengthened the weak, healed the sick, or bound up the injured. You have not brought back the strays or searched for the lost. You have ruled them harshly and brutally."

A shepherd's heart is characterized by humility, compassion, and a genuine love for the flock. They lead by example, demonstrating a life of integrity, devotion, and service. Their greatest joy is to see the sheep flourish and grow in their faith.

Transformative Questions:

1. How does Jesus' example as the Good Shepherd inspire you in your understanding of pastoral leadership?

   _____

   _____

   _____

2. How can you, as a flock member, support and encourage your pastor in their role as a shepherd?

   _____

   _____

3. How can you cultivate a shepherd's heart in your own life, even if you are not in a pastoral role?

   _____

   _____

   _____

Prayer Prompt:

Pray for your pastor and other church leaders that God would grant them a shepherd's heart filled with love, wisdom, and courage to lead the flock according to His will.

Chapter 5:
The Hireling's Agenda

While the Good Shepherd prioritizes the care and spiritual growth of the flock, the hireling has a very different focus. Jesus clearly warns us about such individuals in John 10:12-13: *"The hired hand is not the shepherd and does not own the sheep. So when he sees the wolf coming, he abandons the sheep and runs away. Then, the wolf attacks the flock and scatters it. The man runs away because he is a hired hand and cares nothing for the sheep."*

The hireling's agenda centers on personal gain rather than the flock's well-being. Their focus may include:

Recognition and Reputation: Instead of glorifying Christ, the hireling seeks to build a name for themselves, cultivating a following or achieving celebrity status in ministry.

Material Gain: While the laborer is worthy of their wages (1 Timothy 5:18), hirelings often exploit the flock for financial gain, prioritizing their comfort over kingdom work.

Power and Influence: Hirelings may use their position to wield authority, often at the expense of the congregation's spiritual growth.

This agenda is dangerous because it shifts the church's focus from authentic discipleship to superficial growth metrics. Instead of seeking to nurture spiritual health, the hireling may prioritize the following:

Attendance Numbers: By treating church growth as a business goal, they may prioritize numerical growth above individual spiritual well-being.

Programs Over People: Hirelings might emphasize elaborate events and programs but neglect the genuine needs of the congregation.

Comfort Over Commitment: They often avoid challenging biblical truths to keep the flock comfortable, thus preventing the growth that comes from embracing hard truths.

The church suffers when hirelings lead. The flock becomes vulnerable, scattered, and disillusioned, and the true mission of the church—making disciples—is lost.

Transformative Questions:

1. How can you distinguish between leaders focused on Christ and those pursuing personal agendas?

   _____

   _____

   _____

2. Have you ever encountered a hireling in ministry, and what impact did it have on the church or community?

   _____

   _____

   _____

3. How can you support godly leaders and hold others accountable to biblical standards?

   _____

   _____

   _____

Prayer Prompt:

Pray for discernment to recognize true shepherds and avoid the influence of hirelings. Ask God to guard His church from leaders who prioritize their own agenda over His mission.

Chapter 6:
Recognizing True Shepherds

Discerning a true shepherd can be challenging in an age where charisma and popularity often overshadow character and humility. However, Scripture provides clear guidelines to help us identify those who lead with the heart of Christ.

1. **Biblical Leadership**:

    True shepherds align their ministry with God's Word. They prioritize teaching and living out Scripture (2 Timothy 3:16-17). Their sermons, decisions, and actions reflect a deep commitment to the truth of God's Word rather than personal opinions or cultural trends.

2. **Servant Leadership**:

    Like Jesus, true shepherds serve their flock with humility and love. They embody Mark 10:45, where Jesus says, *"For even the Son of Man did not come to be served, but to serve, and to give his life as a ransom for many."*

3. **Consistency in Character**:

    Shepherds are imperfect, but their lives should be marked by integrity, humility, and love. 1 Timothy 3:1-7 and Titus 1:6-9 outline the qualifications of godly leaders, emphasizing moral character, faithfulness, and the ability to teach and lead with wisdom.

4. **Focus on Discipleship**:

True shepherds emphasize making disciples, equipping the saints for ministry, and helping believers mature in their faith (Ephesians 4:11-13). They are committed to developing others rather than seeking to expand their influence.

5. **Dependence on Christ**:

Ultimately, a faithful shepherd recognizes that they are under-shepherds, accountable to Christ, the Chief Shepherd (1 Peter 5:4). Their ministry reflects a dependence on God's guidance and the empowerment of the Holy Spirit.

Practical Guidelines for Evaluation:

Examine the Fruit: Matthew 7:16 reminds us, *"You will know them by their fruits."* Look for evidence of spiritual growth, godly character, and a Christ-centered focus in their ministry.

Test the Spirit: 1 John 4:1 advises us to test the spirits to see if they are from God. A true shepherd's ministry will glorify Christ, not themselves.

Engage in Dialogue: Don't hesitate to ask questions or seek clarity about a leader's vision, priorities, or biblical stance.

While evaluating leaders is essential, remember that no human shepherd is perfect. Christ is the ultimate Shepherd, and He alone is infallible. True shepherds point others to Him, relying on His strength and wisdom to lead well.

Transformative Questions:

1. How can you use Scripture to evaluate the leaders in your church?

   _____

   _____

   _____

2. What steps can you take to support and encourage godly leaders in your congregation?

   _____

   _____

   _____

3. How can you remain focused on Christ as the Chief Shepherd, even when human leaders fall short?

   _____

   _____

   _____

Prayer Prompt:

Pray for your church leaders, asking God to guide and strengthen them as they shepherd the flock. Pray they remain focused on Christ and empowered by His Spirit to lead with integrity, wisdom, and love.

Part 3:
Sheep vs. Consumers

The relationship between church members and their shepherds mirrors the biblical imagery of sheep and their shepherds. However, in today's church culture, this relationship is often overshadowed by a consumer-driven mindset that prioritizes individual preferences over spiritual growth and mutual edification. This section explores the biblical role of church members, the dangers of the consumer mentality, and practical ways to cultivate a healthy shepherd-sheep relationship.

Chapter 7:
The Role of the Sheep

The Bible consistently refers to believers as sheep, a metaphor that illustrates our dependence on God, our need for guidance, and our responsibility within the body of Christ. Understanding this role is essential for fostering spiritual growth and unity within the church.

1. **Submission to the Shepherd and Christ**:

   Sheep are called to follow their shepherd's guidance, just as believers are called to follow Christ and support their spiritual leaders. Hebrews 13:17 emphasizes this role: *"Have confidence in your leaders and submit to their authority because they keep watch over you as those who must give an account. Do this so their work will be a joy, not a burden, for that would not benefit you."* Submission is an act of trust and faith, acknowledging the shepherd's God-given responsibility to lead with wisdom and love.

2. **Teachability and Obedience**:

   Sheep must remain teachable and willing to learn and grow under the instruction of their shepherd and the Word of God. Proverbs 19:20 says, *"Listen to advice and accept discipline, and at the end, you will be counted among the wise."* Obedience to biblical teaching is a mark of maturity and an essential aspect of discipleship.

3. **Support for the Shepherd:**

    Sheep have a responsibility to encourage and support their shepherds. Pastors often carry heavy spiritual, emotional, and practical burdens. Galatians 6:6 reminds us, *"Nevertheless, the one who receives instruction in the word should share all good things with their instructor."* Supporting leaders in prayer, service, and encouragement strengthens the church community.

4. **Active Participation in the Flock:**

    Sheep are not passive participants but active contributors to the health and vitality of the flock. Each member has spiritual gifts meant to improve the church (1 Corinthians 12:7). Active participation involves serving others, fostering unity, and building relationships that reflect Christ's love.

Transformative Questions:

1. How does the biblical role of sheep challenge your perspective on your responsibilities within the church?

   _____

   _____

   _____

2. How can you demonstrate submission, obedience, and teachability in your spiritual journey?

   _____

   _____

   _____

3. How are you actively supporting your pastor and engaging with your church community?

   _____

   _____

   _____

Prayer Prompt:

Pray for a heart of submission and teachability. Ask God to help you trust His guidance through spiritual leaders and to strengthen your role within the church body.

Chapter 8:
The Consumer Mindset

In today's church culture, a dangerous trend has emerged—the consumer mindset. This mentality reduces church participation to a transaction where individuals seek to have their preferences met rather than embracing their role as active disciples.

1. **The Problem of Entitlement**:

    The consumer mindset fosters entitlement, where church members expect to have their desires catered to, whether in worship styles, sermon topics, or church programs. This focus on individual preferences often leads to discontentment and division within the body of Christ.

2. **The "Church Shopping" Mentality**:

    Many believers approach church selection as shopping for a product, seeking congregations that entertain, comfort, or align with personal tastes. This consumeristic approach prioritizes convenience over commitment and spiritual growth.

3. **The Impact on Church Culture**:

    When the church caters to the consumer mentality, its mission shifts from discipleship to performance. Churches may focus on attendance numbers, elaborate programs, or maintaining the comfort of their members rather than challenging them to grow in faith and fulfill the Great Commission.

4. **Abandoning the Consumer Mentality**:

To combat the consumer mindset, believers must shift their focus from "What can the church do for me?" to "How can I serve the church and God's kingdom?" Romans 12:1-2 reminds us to present ourselves as living sacrifices, renewing our minds to align with God's purpose. Spiritual growth comes through commitment, service, and surrender, not personal comfort.

Transformative Questions:

1. Have you ever approached the church with a consumer mindset? How has it affected your spiritual growth?

    _____

    _____

    _____

2. What steps can you take to prioritize spiritual growth over personal preferences in your church participation?

    _____

    _____

    _____

3. How can you challenge others to abandon the consumer mentality and embrace their role in the body of Christ?

    _____

    _____

    _____

Prayer Prompt:

Pray for a heart of humility and commitment. Ask God to reveal areas where you may have prioritized personal desires over spiritual growth and to help you embrace a selfless attitude in serving His church.

Chapter 9:
Cultivating a Shepherd-Sheep Relationship

A healthy relationship between pastors and church members is foundational to a congregation's spiritual health. This relationship must be built on mutual trust, respect, and shared commitment to Christ's mission.

1. **Open Communication:**

   Just as shepherds listen to the needs of their sheep, pastors rely on honest feedback from their congregation. Members should feel free to share their concerns, questions, and encouragement with their leaders in a spirit of love and respect (Ephesians 4:15).

2. **Mutual Respect and Support:**

   Both shepherds and sheep must respect one another's roles within the church. Pastors are called to lead with humility and wisdom, while members are called to support their leaders through prayer, encouragement, and active participation (1 Thessalonians 5:12-13).

3. **Accountability and Guidance:**

   Accountability is essential in the shepherd-sheep relationship. Pastors are accountable to God and their congregation, while church members are accountable to their spiritual leaders. This mutual accountability fosters spiritual growth and ensures the church remains focused on Christ's mission.

4. **Shared Mission**:

A healthy shepherd-sheep relationship thrives when pastors and members unite to fulfill the Great Commission. When the flock and its leaders work together, the church becomes a powerful force for God's kingdom.

Transformative Questions:

1. How can you contribute to a healthy relationship between pastors and members of your church?

   _____

   _____

   _____

2. What steps can you take to foster open communication and mutual respect in your congregation?

   _____

   _____

   _____

3. How does accountability strengthen the spiritual health of both pastors and members?

   _____

   _____

   _____

Prayer Prompt:

Pray for your pastor and church leaders. Ask God to bless their ministry, guide their decisions, and strengthen their relationship with the congregation. Pray for unity and shared commitment to Christ's mission within your church.

Part 4:
Christ, the Head of the Church

The church must reflect Christ's kingdom on earth, but many congregations unintentionally shift their focus to human leaders, programs, and traditions. This section redirects attention to Jesus as the true Head of the church and explores how to align with His teachings, avoid harmful leadership dynamics, and rely on the Holy Spirit's guidance.

Chapter 10:
Remembering Our True Leader

Christ as the Head

Christ is the foundation and ongoing leader of the church. Paul emphasizes in Colossians 1:18, *"And He is the head of the body, the church; He is the beginning and the firstborn from among the dead, so that in everything He might have the supremacy."*

> **What it looks like** A Christ-centered church constantly points its members back to Jesus. The pastor regularly emphasizes Christ's teachings over personal anecdotes or opinions in sermons. Worship songs glorify Jesus rather than focusing solely on individual experiences. Church decisions are made prayerfully, seeking His will.

The Problem of Human Leadership Superseding Christ

Churches sometimes emphasize a pastor's charisma or a denomination's traditions more than Christ Himself. Matthew 23:8-10 warns, *"You are not to be called 'Rabbi,' for you have one Teacher, and you are all brothers."*

> **What it looks like** Members quote their pastor more than they quote Scripture. A congregation might split over a pas-

tor's departure, revealing misplaced loyalty. Programs or traditions may become so rigid that they overshadow the church's mission to reflect Jesus.

Renewed Focus on Scripture

Christ's teachings must remain the ultimate authority. John 8:31-32 reminds us, *"If you hold to My teaching, you are My disciples. Then you will know the truth, and the truth will set you free."*

What it looks like is Bible studies and small groups that dive deeply into Scripture, equipping members to discern the truth. The church provides resources like devotionals and encourages members to read the Bible independently.

Transformative Questions

1. How does your church keep Christ central to its teaching and activities?

_____

_____

_____

2. How can you ensure your walk prioritizes Jesus' teachings?

_____

_____

_____

3. How can your church encourage Scripture-based discipleship over traditions or human opinions?

_____

_____

_____

Prayer Prompt

Pray for your church to embrace Christ as its true leader. Ask God to guide decisions, align activities with His will, and strengthen your personal focus on Jesus.

Chapter 11:
The Dangers of "My Pastor Said"

The Risk of Blindly Following Pastors

While pastors are vital spiritual leaders, they are fallible. Believers are called to test all teachings against Scripture, as seen in Acts 17:11: *"The Berean Jews were of more noble character... for they received the message with great eagerness and examined the Scriptures every day to see if what Paul said was true."*

> **What it looks like** A church member who hears a sermon cross-references the Scripture passages to ensure alignment. Leaders encourage questions rather than discourage discussion. Congregants pray for understanding and discernment after each message.

Developing Personal Discernment

A personal relationship with Christ allows believers to hear His voice. James 1:5 assures, *"If any of you lacks wisdom, you should ask God, who gives generously to all without finding fault, and it will be given to you."*

> **What it looks like**: Members make decisions in their personal lives (e.g., career changes, family conflicts) by seeking

God through prayer and Scripture rather than solely relying on a pastor's advice.

Avoiding the "Cult of Personality"

Excessive admiration of pastors can create a "cult of personality," where the leader overshadows Christ. Paul rebuked this in 1 Corinthians 1:12-13: *"One of you says, 'I follow Paul'; another, 'I follow Apollos.' Is Christ divided?"*

> **What it looks like** is a church where members follow Christ rather than align with factions around specific leaders. Leadership transitions occur smoothly because loyalty lies with Christ, not an individual.

Transformative Questions

1. How can you balance respect for pastors with a commitment to biblical discernment?

   _____

   _____

   _____

2. Have you relied on a pastor's advice over seeking God's guidance directly?

   _____

   _____

   _____

3. What safeguards can you and your church implement to ensure Christ remains central?

Prayer Prompt

Pray for discernment and wisdom to evaluate teachings against Scripture. Ask God to protect your church from idolatry and to strengthen your relationship with Him.

Chapter 12:
Operating Under the Holy Spirit's Influence

The Spirit vs. Human Strategies

The early church succeeded because it relied on the Holy Spirit, not marketing strategies or human efforts. Zechariah 4:6 declares, *"'Not by might nor by power, but by My Spirit,' says the Lord Almighty."*

> **What it looks like** A church that prioritizes prayer meetings over promotional campaigns. Ministry decisions are based on prayerful discernment and the Spirit's leading, not business growth models. For example, a church plants a new ministry because members feel led by the Spirit, not because it's a trendy idea.

Prayer and Seeking God's Will

Prayer is the lifeline of a Spirit-led church. Acts 4:31 shows the power of prayer: *"After they prayed, the place where they were meeting was shaken. And they were all filled with the Holy Spirit and boldly spoke God's word."*

> **What it looks like** Leaders call for fasting and prayer before making significant decisions. Church members regularly pray for their community, ministries, and one anoth-

er. Worship services include dedicated times for corporate prayer and listening for the Spirit's voice.

Evaluating Church Activities

Churches must assess their programs to ensure they align with biblical principles and reflect God's mission. Galatians 5:25 calls believers to *"keep in step with the Spirit."*

> **What it looks like** Ministries are evaluated not by attendance numbers but by spiritual fruit, such as changed lives, stronger faith, and deeper relationships with Christ. A church may end a popular but spiritually shallow program to focus on discipleship and outreach.

Transformative Questions

1. How does your church prioritize the Holy Spirit's guidance over worldly strategies?

   _____

   _____

   _____

2. How can you personally contribute to fostering a Spirit-led culture in your church?

   _____

   _____

   _____

3. What activities or programs in your church reflect God's will, and which might need reevaluation?

   _____

   _____

   _____

Prayer Prompt

Pray for a fresh outpouring of the Holy Spirit in your church. Ask God to guide leaders, align activities with His will, and empower the congregation to fulfill His mission.

*This section reinforces **Christ's authority as the true Head of the church**, highlights the dangers of misplaced trust in human leadership, and emphasizes the necessity of Holy Spirit-led ministry.*

Part 5:
The Church's Mission: Making Disciples

The church's ultimate mission, as entrusted by Jesus, is to make disciples of all nations. However, in many modern contexts, the focus has shifted from discipleship to programs, entertainment, and competition. This section challenges readers to reclaim the Great Commission, prioritize unity among believers, and realign church activities to foster spiritual growth and send out equipped disciples.

Chapter 13:
Reclaiming the Great Commission

Christ's Command to Make Disciples

The Great Commission, found in Matthew 28:19-20, is the cornerstone of the church's mission: *"Therefore go and make disciples of all nations, baptizing them in the name of the Father and of the Son and the Holy Spirit, and teaching them to obey everything I have commanded you. And surely I am with you always, to the very end of the age."* Making disciples is not optional—it is a command that extends to every believer.

> **What it looks like**: A church prioritizing discipleship may organize small groups where members are taught to study Scripture deeply, apply it, and mentor others in their faith journey. Members are encouraged to share their faith actively in their communities and workplaces, not just rely on bringing people to church events.

From Attracting Members to Sending Out Disciples

Modern churches often focus on increasing attendance rather than equipping members to fulfill the Great Commission. Ephesians

4:11-12 reminds us, *"So Christ Himself gave the apostles, the prophets, the evangelists, the pastors, and teachers, to equip His people for works of service, so that the body of Christ may be built up."*

> **What it looks like**: A church actively trains its congregation to serve outside its walls. For example, members may be trained to lead Bible studies in their neighborhoods or participate in mission trips to unreached areas.

Active Participation in Evangelism and Discipleship

Every believer has a role in making disciples. Acts 1:8 declares, *"But you will receive power when the Holy Spirit comes on you, and you will be my witnesses in Jerusalem, and in all Judea and Samaria, and to the ends of the earth."*

> **What it looks like** is that members share testimonies of their faith during services and are encouraged to engage in relational evangelism, which builds authentic relationships to share the Gospel naturally. New believers are paired with mentors who guide them in their spiritual growth.

Transformative Questions

1. How does your church equip members to participate in the Great Commission?

    _____

    _____

    _____

2. In what ways are you personally engaging in evangelism and discipleship?

    _____

    _____

    _____

3. What steps can you take to move from being a church attendee to an active disciple-maker?

    _____

    _____

    _____

Prayer Prompt

Pray for God to give you a heart for discipleship and the courage to share your faith. Ask Him to guide your church in equipping and sending out disciples who will impact the world for Christ.

Chapter 14:
Addressing the Issue of Competition

The Problem of Church Competition

Competition between churches and denominations often distracts from the shared mission of spreading the Gospel. Jesus prayed for unity among His followers in John 17:21: *"That all of them may be one, Father, just as You are in Me and I am in You. May they also be in Us so that the world may believe that You have sent Me."*

> **What it looks like**: Churches in the same city compete to attract members by offering flashier programs or bigger events instead of partnering to address community needs or reach the lost.

Fostering Unity Among Believers

Paul reminds us in 1 Corinthians 12:12, *"Just as a body, though one, has many parts, but all its many parts form one body, so it is with Christ."* Unity among believers strengthens the church's ability to fulfill its mission.

> **What it looks like** Local churches collaborating on service projects, such as feeding the hungry or providing disaster relief, to show the love of Christ to their community. Pastors

from different denominations meet to pray together and discuss ways to work cooperatively.

The True Enemy

Ephesians 6:12 reminds us of our real battle: *"For our struggle is not against flesh and blood, but against the rulers, against the authorities, against the powers of this dark world and against the spiritual forces of evil in the heavenly realms."*

What it looks like is A church that focuses on spiritual warfare through prayer, fasting, and teaching about the power of the Gospel to overcome sin and darkness rather than competing with other churches for influence or recognition.

Transformative Questions

1. How has competition between churches impacted your view of the body of Christ?

_____

_____

_____

2. What steps can you take to foster unity with other believers and congregations?

_____

_____

_____

3. How can your church refocus its energy on the shared mission of advancing the Gospel?

_____

_____

_____

Prayer Prompt

Pray for unity within the body of Christ. Ask God to break down barriers between churches and denominations, fostering cooperation and shared commitment to His mission.

Chapter 15:
Rethinking Church Activities

The Problem with Entertainment-Driven Ministry

Many churches rely heavily on entertainment and flashy programs to attract people. While these may draw crowds, they often fail to produce genuine discipleship. Paul warns in 2 Timothy 4:3-4, *"For the time will come when people will not put up with sound doctrine. Instead, to suit their own desires, they will gather around them a great number of teachers to say what their itching ears want to hear."*

> **What it looks like** Churches prioritizing elaborate productions or events over teaching sound doctrine. Members may attend for the excitement but need a deeper understanding of Scripture or commitment to Christ.

Prioritizing Spiritual Growth Over Programs

Church activities should foster spiritual growth and discipleship, not just entertain or retain members. Hebrews 10:24-25 encourages believers to focus on spiritual accountability: *"And let us consider how we may spur one another on toward love and good deeds, not giving up meeting together... but encouraging one another."*

What it looks like is A church that scales back on entertainment-driven events and focuses on activities like prayer meetings, in-depth Bible studies, and service projects. For example, the church may organize a community prayer walk or a Scripture memorization challenge instead of a large concert.

Evaluating Activities Against Biblical Principles

Churches must assess their activities to ensure they align with their mission. Matthew 7:16 reminds us, *"By their fruit, you will recognize them."*

What it looks like is that Leaders review church programs to determine if they lead to measurable spiritual growth, such as increased Bible knowledge, deeper prayer lives, or more members actively sharing their faith. Ministries that don't produce fruit may be restructured or replaced.

Transformative Questions

1. How do the activities in your church contribute to genuine spiritual growth?

_____

_____

_____

2. Are there any church programs that prioritize entertainment over discipleship?

_____

_____

_____

3. What steps can you take to encourage your church to prioritize spiritual transformation?

_____

_____

_____

Prayer Prompt

Pray for your church to prioritize activities that lead to spiritual growth and genuine discipleship. Ask God to guide leaders in evaluating programs and to inspire creativity in fostering transformation.

*This section challenges churches and individuals to **refocus on making disciples,** fostering unity, and prioritizing spiritual growth over entertainment.*

Conclusion:
A Transformative Call to Action

The Church's Mission: A Sacred Responsibility

At the heart of this book lies an urgent and transformative truth: the church's primary mission is to make disciples, not members. Jesus' Great Commission in Matthew 28:19-20 commands, *"Therefore go and make disciples of all nations, baptizing them in the name of the Father and of the Son and the Holy Spirit, and teaching them to obey everything I have commanded you. And surely I am with you always, to the very end of the age."* This call is not optional. It is the lifeblood of the church's purpose, yet it is often lost amid programs, traditions, and worldly distractions.

A Renewed Perspective

Paul's appeal in Romans 12:1-2 sets the foundation for transformation:

"Therefore, I urge you, brothers and sisters, in view of God's mercy, to offer your bodies as a living sacrifice, holy and pleasing to God—this is your true and proper worship. Do not conform to the pattern of this world, but be transformed by the renewing of your mind. Then you will be able to test and approve what God's will is—His good, pleasing, and perfect will."

The church must resist the patterns of the world—consumerism, competition, and entertainment-driven ministry—and embrace the renewing power of God's Spirit. This transformation begins with a commitment to live as disciples and to make disciples, fulfilling Christ's command.

A Call to Pastors and Leaders

Reexamine Your Role as Shepherds

As spiritual leaders, pastors guide the flock toward Christ and His mission. The Great Commission is not about building personal platforms or filling pews but equipping believers to live as disciple-makers. Ephesians 4:11-12 reminds us, *"So Christ Himself gave the apostles, the prophets, the evangelists, the pastors, and teachers, to equip His people for works of service, so that the body of Christ may be built up."*

> **Action Step**: Assess your church's activities and programs. Do they align to make disciples? Are you equipping your congregation to grow in their faith and share the Gospel? If not, it's time to restructure priorities.

> **Encouragement**: Trust in God's promise that He will guide your steps as you realign with His will. Proverbs 3:5-6 says, *"Trust in the Lord with all your heart and lean not on your understanding; in all your ways submit to Him, and He will make your paths straight."*

A Call to Church Members

Rediscover Your Role as Disciple

Every believer is called to be a disciple and a disciple-maker. This means living out your faith daily, seeking a deeper relationship with Christ, and sharing the hope of the Gospel with others. Acts 1:8 reminds us, *"But you will receive power when the Holy Spirit comes on you; and you will be my witnesses in Jerusalem, and in all Judea and Samaria, and to the ends of the earth."*

> **Action Step**: Commit to daily prayer practices, Bible study, and obedience to God's Word. Seek opportunities to mentor new believers and share your faith with those around you.

> **Encouragement**: You don't need to be perfect or have all the answers. Trust in the Holy Spirit's power to guide and equip you for the mission. Philippians 4:13 declares, *"I can do all this through Him who gives me strength."*

A Call to the Whole Church

Unite for the Mission

Competition between churches and denominations weakens the body of Christ. The mission of the Gospel is too urgent for division. Jesus prayed for unity in John 17:21: *"That all of them may be one, Father, just as You are in Me and I am in You. May they also be in Us so that the world may believe that You have sent Me."*

Action Step: Partner with other local churches to serve your community. Collaborate on evangelistic efforts and share resources to reach more people with the Gospel.

Encouragement: When believers unite in unity, God's power is magnified. Psalm 133:1 says, *"How good and pleasant it is when God's people live together in unity!"*

Hope for Revival and Renewal

Despite the challenges facing the modern church, God is still at work. Revival and renewal are possible when His people humble themselves, seek His face, and commit to His mission. 2 Chronicles 7:14 offers a promise: *"If My people, who are called by My name, will humble themselves and pray and seek My face and turn from their wicked ways, then I will hear from heaven, and I will forgive their sin and will heal their land."*

Encouragement: Trust that God is faithful to bring about His purposes. Isaiah 55:11 assures us, *"So is My word that goes out from My mouth: It will not return to Me empty, but will accomplish what I desire and achieve the purpose for which I sent it.*

Relevant Scriptures for Study

The Bible is the ultimate authority and guide for understanding and fulfilling the Great Commission. These passages serve as foundational texts for believers who desire to grow in their faith and advance God's kingdom.

1. The Great Commission

Matthew 28:19-20: Jesus commands His disciples to make disciples of all nations. This is the core mission of the church, calling every believer to participate in sharing the Gospel and teaching others.

Mark 16:15: Jesus extends the call to proclaim the Gospel to all creation, emphasizing the universal nature of His mission.

Luke 24:46-49: Jesus promises the power of the Holy Spirit to equip believers for their mission.

Acts 1:8: Jesus instructs His followers to be witnesses locally and globally, empowered by the Holy Spirit.

Why These Are Important: These scriptures clarify the church's purpose and empower believers to act boldly, trusting in Jesus' authority and promise of His presence.

2. Unity and Cooperation

John 17:20-23: Jesus prays for unity among believers, showing that our oneness reflects God's love for the world.

Ephesians 4:3-6: Paul emphasizes the unity of the Spirit and the oneness of the body of Christ.

1 Corinthians 12:12-14: Like a body, the church consists of many parts working together for God's glory.

Why These Are Important: Unity strengthens the church's ability to fulfill its mission and demonstrates Christ's love for the world.

3. **Discipleship**

   Luke 9:23-24: Jesus calls His followers to take up their cross daily, illustrating the cost of discipleship.

   John 8:31-32: Abiding in Jesus' teachings is the hallmark of true discipleship.

   2 Timothy 2:2: Paul instructs Timothy to entrust the Gospel to faithful people who will continue the mission.

   Why These Are Important: Discipleship is growing in Christ, and equipping others to do the same ensures the multiplication of faithful believers.

4. **Evangelism**

   Romans 10:14-15: The necessity of preaching the Gospel so others may hear and believe.

   2 Corinthians 5:20: Believers are ambassadors for Christ, representing Him to the world.

   1 Peter 3:15: The call to always be prepared to give an answer for the hope we have in Christ.

   Why These Are Important: Evangelism is the outward expression of our faith, bringing the message of salvation to a lost world.

Prayer Guides

1. **Prayers for the Great Commission**

   Pray for laborers (Matthew 9:37-38).

   Pray for boldness (Acts 4:29).

   Pray for the lost (1 Timothy 2:1-4).

   Why This Is Important: These focused prayers align your heart with God's mission, interceding for the spread of the Gospel and the empowerment of believers.

2. **30-Day Prayer Guide for Revival**

3. **Why This Is Important**: This guide offers prayers focused on personal transformation, church renewal, and community impact.

4. **Acts Model of Prayer**:

   Adoration, Confession, Thanksgiving, Supplication.

   Why This Is Important: A balanced prayer life fosters a deeper relationship with God and covers all aspects of worship and intercession.

Action Plans: A Blueprint for Living Out the Great Commission

Action plans are practical, step-by-step strategies designed to help you apply what you've learned in this book or journal to real-life situations. They bridge the gap between reflection and action, ensuring that the principles of discipleship, leadership, and service move from the pages of your journal into tangible, impactful steps.

Why Action Plans Are Important

1. Turn Intentions Into Actions:

Without a clear plan, it's easy to feel inspired but unsure of how to proceed. Action plans provide clarity and direction, helping you take practical steps toward fulfilling the Great Commission.

2. Build Accountability:

Writing down specific actions makes you more likely to follow through. Sharing your plans with a trusted friend, mentor, or small group creates an added layer of accountability and encouragement.

3. Measure Growth and Impact:

Action plans give you a way to track your progress and celebrate milestones along the journey. They help you see how God is working through your obedience, whether in small daily steps or significant ministry decisions.

4. Align with Biblical Principles:

Scripture calls us to not only hear God's Word but to act on it (James 1:22). Action plans ensure that your learning translates into faithful obedience to God's call.

How Action Plans Work

Each action plan is tailored to your role—whether you are an individual believer, a church leader, or a seasoned disciple. They are designed to align with the themes of discipleship, evangelism, unity, and service. Here's what an action plan typically includes:

1. Define Your Mission:

Start by clarifying your goal, such as mentoring someone in faith, organizing an outreach event, or fostering unity in your church.

2. Set Specific Steps:

Break down your mission into smaller, actionable steps. For example, if your goal is to mentor someone, your steps might include praying for God's guidance, identifying a mentee, and setting up a regular meeting schedule.

3. Identify Resources and Support:

Determine what tools, resources, or people you'll need to succeed. This might include study materials, prayer support, or involvement from church leadership.

4. Set a Timeline:

Assign realistic deadlines for each step to maintain momentum.

5. Pray and Act:

Commit your plan to prayer, asking God for wisdom, guidance, and strength. Then take the first step, trusting that He will equip you for what lies ahead.

Personal Action Plan

For individuals desiring to align their lives with Christ's mission and grow as disciples.

1. Evaluate Your Walk with Christ

Define Your Mission: Deepen your relationship with Christ by identifying areas in need of spiritual growth.

Steps:

1. Spend time in prayer, asking God to reveal areas where you need to grow.

2. Reflect on your habits and priorities—are they aligned with God's will?

3. Write down two specific changes you can make to grow closer to Him.

Why This Is Important: Transformation begins with self-awareness and a willingness to align your life with God's will (Romans 12:1-2).

2. Engage in Discipleship

Define Your Mission: Commit to spiritual growth through mentorship and community.

Steps:

1. Seek a mentor who can guide you in your faith journey.

2. Join a small group or Bible study focused on discipleship.

3. Identify someone you can disciple or encourage in their faith.

Why This Is Important: Discipleship ensures spiritual multiplication, equipping others to carry out the church's mission (2 Timothy 2:2).

3. Be Intentional in Evangelism

Define Your Mission: Share the Gospel with those who need hope and salvation.

Steps:

1. Pray daily for at least one person who doesn't know Christ.

2. Build relationships with non-believers through acts of kindness and genuine conversations.

3. Commit to sharing the Gospel with at least one person each week.

Why This Is Important: Evangelism is the heartbeat of the Great Commission, bringing hope and salvation to a lost world (Matthew 28:19-20).

Church Action Plan for Leaders (Pastors)

For pastors and leaders entrusted with guiding the body of Christ.

1. Evaluate the Church's Ministries

Define Your Mission: Ensure every ministry aligns with the mission of making disciples.

Steps:

1. Conduct a ministry audit to assess whether programs foster discipleship and spiritual growth.

2. Eliminate or restructure ministries that do not align with the Great Commission.

3. Set measurable goals, such as mentoring new believers or increasing outreach efforts.

Why This Is Important: Ministries should equip the congregation to make disciples, not distract from the church's primary mission (Ephesians 4:11-12).

2. Develop a Discipleship Pathway

Define Your Mission: Create a clear process for members to grow in their faith.

Steps:

1. Design a step-by-step discipleship process, including paths for new and mature believers.

2. Offer resources such as Bible studies, mentorship opportunities, and growth workshops.

3. Regularly communicate the pathway to the congregation and encourage participation.

Why This Is Important: A clear discipleship pathway ensures members know how to grow in their faith and fulfill their calling (Colossians 1:28).

3. Equip the Congregation for Evangelism

Define Your Mission: Empower members to share the Gospel confidently.

Steps:

1. Organize training sessions on evangelism and mentoring.

2. Provide practical tools such as Gospel tracts, conversation starters, and digital resources.

3. Celebrate testimonies of evangelism and discipleship during church services.

Why This Is Important: Equipping the congregation empowers the church to fulfill the Great Commission together rather than relying solely on leaders (Acts 1:8).

4. Foster Unity and Collaboration

Define Your Mission: Build relationships within the church and across the broader Christian community.

Steps:

1. Partner with other local churches for outreach events, prayer gatherings, and service projects.

2. Host church-wide activities that encourage unity, such as meals or worship nights.

3. Meet with leaders from other denominations to discuss opportunities for collaboration.

Why This Is Important: Unity strengthens the church's witness to the world and maximizes its impact (John 17:21).

5. Model Commitment to the Mission

Define Your Mission: Inspire members by living out the Great Commission authentically.

Steps:

1. Lead by example in personal evangelism, prayer, and discipleship.

2. Share personal testimonies of how you are fulfilling Christ's mission.

3. Regularly evaluate your own spiritual walk and make adjustments as needed.

Why This Is Important: Members are more likely to embrace the mission when they see their leaders living it authentically (1 Corinthians 11:1).

Church Action Plan for Members (Seasoned Disciples)

For seasoned believers ready to live out their calling as disciple-makers.

1. Commit to Personal Discipleship

Define Your Mission: Strengthen your relationship with Christ.

Steps:

1. Spend time daily in prayer, Bible study, and reflection.

2. Join a small group or accountability partner to encourage mutual growth.

3. Memorize a scripture each week to deepen your understanding of God's Word.

Why This Is Important: Personal discipleship equips you to grow your faith and effectively disciple others (2 Peter 3:18).

2. Engage in Evangelism

Define Your Mission: Boldly share your faith with others.

Steps:

1. Pray for three people who need to know Christ and look for opportunities to share the Gospel.

2. Use church-provided resources, such as tracts or online tools, to start conversations.

3. Share your testimony with someone this month.

Why This Is Important: Evangelism spreads the Gospel to those who need hope, fulfilling Christ's command (Mark 16:15).

3. Serve in Ministry

Define Your Mission: Use your gifts to serve the church and community.

Steps:

1. Identify your spiritual gifts through prayer or a church assessment.

2. Volunteer in a ministry that aligns with your gifts and passions.

3. Participate in community service projects organized by your church.

Why This Is Important: Serving in ministry demonstrates God's love in action and contributes to the church's mission (1 Peter 4:10).

4. Support Your Leaders

Define Your Mission: Encourage and pray for your pastors and church leaders.

Steps:

1. Pray weekly for your leaders, asking God to guide, protect, and strengthen them.

2. Offer encouragement through notes, feedback, or volunteering where needed.

3. Support their vision by participating actively in church initiatives.

Why This Is Important: Supporting leaders fosters unity and ensures they are equipped to shepherd effectively (Hebrews 13:17).

5. Be a Disciple-Maker

Define Your Mission: Multiply your faith by mentoring others.

Steps:

1. Identify someone in your church or community to mentor or disciple.

2. Meet regularly to study scripture, pray, and encourage one another.

3. Encourage them to repeat the process by discipling someone else.

Why This Is Important: Discipleship ensures that Christ's mission continues to multiply and grow, fulfilling His command to make disciples of all nations (Matthew 28:19-20).

These action plans are tools for transformation. Commit to them, pray over them, and trust God to work through your obedience!

Final Note:

Pastors and members working together as a unified body can accomplish extraordinary things for the kingdom of God. When leaders model commitment and equip their congregations, and when members actively live out their faith, the church becomes a powerful force for transformation in the world.

Additional Resources
for Further Growth

The Bible: Your Primary Resource

Before diving into any supplemental materials, remember that the Bible is the ultimate resource for understanding and living out the Great Commission. Scripture is God's Word, inspired and sufficient for equipping believers to serve Him faithfully (2 Timothy 3:16-17). Let the Bible be your foundation for every reflection, decision, and action as you grow in discipleship, leadership, and unity in the body of Christ.

To enhance your study of the Bible, consider using these additional resources that complement and reinforce biblical truths. These books provide practical insights, inspiration, and guidance for living as a disciple and disciple-maker.

Books on Personal Discipleship

1. **Experiencing God: Knowing and Doing the Will of God** by Henry T. Blackaby and Claude V. King

   □ A transformative guide to recognizing God's activity in your life and responding to His call. This book encourages intimacy with God as the foundation for discipleship.

2. **The Pursuit of God** by A.W. Tozer

□ A devotional classic that emphasizes the importance of seeking a deeper relationship with God through surrender and focus on His presence.

3. **Follow Me: A Call to Die. A Call to Live.** by David Platt

□ A bold reminder of the cost and joy of following Jesus, inspiring believers to live fully as His disciples.

Books on Leadership and Ministry

4. **Spiritual Leadership: Moving People on to God's Agenda** by Henry T. Blackaby and Richard Blackaby

□ A must-read for pastors and leaders, focusing on leading with humility, reliance on God, and alignment with His purposes.

5. **The Emotionally Healthy Leader** by Peter Scazzero

□ A guide to developing emotional and spiritual maturity for sustainable, effective leadership in ministry.

6. **Canoeing the Mountains: Christian Leadership in Uncharted Territory** by Tod Bolsinger

□ A compelling book for leaders navigating the challenges of ministry in a rapidly changing world, offering practical strategies and encouragement.

Books on Evangelism and the Great Commission

7. **Seeking Him: Experiencing the Joy of Personal Revival**
   by Nancy Leigh DeMoss and Tim Grissom

   ❑ This book emphasizes personal and church-wide revival through repentance, renewal, and intimacy with God.

8. **The Master Plan of Evangelism** by Robert E. Coleman

   ❑ A timeless classic on Jesus' method of disciple-making, offering a simple, effective framework for evangelism.

9. **Evangelism in a Skeptical World** by Sam Chan

   ❑ A practical guide to sharing the Gospel effectively in today's pluralistic and often skeptical culture.

Books for Church Members and Discipleship Teams

10. **Discipleship Essentials: A Guide to Building Your Life in Christ** by Greg Ogden

    A workbook for individuals, small groups, or mentorship relationships to develop spiritual maturity and accountability.

11. **Multiply: Disciples Making Disciples** by Francis Chan and Mark Beuving

A simple yet profound challenge for every believer to embrace the call to make disciples and live as Christ's followers.

12. **Life Together: The Classic Exploration of Christian Community** by Dietrich Bonhoeffer

A powerful exploration of the significance of fellowship and community in the life of believers.

Books on Unity and the Church

13. **The Peacemaker: A Biblical Guide to Resolving Personal Conflict** by Ken Sande

A practical resource for fostering peace and reconciliation within the church, grounded in biblical principles.

14. **Love Your Church: 8 Great Things About Being a Church Member** by Tony Merida

☐ An inspiring book that celebrates the beauty of the local church and encourages active, joyful membership.

15. **Unity in Action: Building Stronger Church Communities** by Various Authors

☐ A practical guide for building unity, collaboration, and purpose within the body of Christ.

These resources are designed to complement and reinforce your Bible study. Use them individually or in group settings to deepen your understanding and application of discipleship, leadership, and unity in your walk with Christ. Let the Bible remain your foundation, and allow these tools to enhance your journey as you seek to fulfill the Great Commission.

A Final Word of Encouragement

The journey of transformation is not one of perfection but of surrender and faithfulness. God calls each of us to offer ourselves as living sacrifices, holy and pleasing to Him (Romans 12:1-2). When we renew our minds through His Word and embrace His mission, we become vessels of His power and glory.

Revival and renewal are possible in the church today. As individuals and congregations align with the Great Commission, God will work through us to bring hope, healing, and salvation to the world.

Prayer

Heavenly Father, thank You for the gift of Your Son and the privilege of participating in Your mission. Help us to live as living sacrifices, holy and pleasing to You. Renew our minds, align our hearts with Your purposes, and empower us to make disciples. Unite Your church in love and cooperation, and revive our hearts, communities, and the world. May everything we do glorify You and advance Your kingdom. In Jesus' name, amen.

Meet the Author

Alisa Ladawn Grace is an accomplished author, educator, and life coach whose work centers on spiritual renewal, personal growth, and living out the transformative power of faith. With a Specialist Degree in Curriculum and Instruction and years of experience as a school administrator and nonprofit leader, Alisa brings her passion for education and her deep commitment to Christ into every book she writes.

Her latest book, *Where Are the Fishers of Men? The Great Commission: Lost in the Crowd!*, is a heartfelt and thought-provoking call to rediscover the essence of discipleship. Challenging the modern church's focus on programs and preferences, Alisa calls pastors, leaders, and believers to reclaim the mission of making disciples of all nations. With biblical truths, practical insights, and actionable guidance, this book empowers readers to live out the Great Commission and bring the hope of Christ to a world in need.

Alisa's previous works reflect her commitment to spiritual transformation and personal renewal. In *No Turning Back: Breaking Free from the Grip of Yesterday*, she helps readers release past hurts and step into a life of freedom and purpose. In *Renewed: The Transformational Power of Putting Off the Old and Putting On the New*, she inspires individuals to embrace Christ-like virtues and experience spiritual renewal grounded in Ephesians 4:22-24.

Alisa's other impactful titles, including *Spirit Empowered: Living a Life of Grace, Compassion, and Forgiveness*, guide readers to overcome life's challenges through the Holy Spirit's power, while *Unlocking Your Great Potential* equips individuals with the tools to thrive emotionally, spiritually, and practically.

Her writing is marked by heartfelt storytelling, scriptural exploration, and a clear call to action. Alisa's mission is to help individuals and churches alike rediscover their purpose, align their hearts with God's will, and live out the transformative power of the Gospel.

Through her books, coaching, and leadership, Alisa Ladawn Grace continues to inspire and equip readers to grow in faith, deepen their discipleship, and live lives that reflect the heart of Christ's mission.